ST JOHN MARY VIANNEY, THE CURÉ OF ARS

St John Mary Vianney, the Curé of Ars

A Parish Priest for all the World

ST PAULS

ST PAULS Publishing
187 Battersea Bridge Road, London SW11 3AS, UK
www.stpaulspublishing.com

Copyright © St Pauls Publishing 2009
ISBN 978-0-85439-765-5

A catalogue record is available for this book from the British Library.

Set by Tukan DTP, Stubbington, Fareham, UK
Printed by AGAM, Cuneo, Italy

ST PAULS is an activity of the priests and brothers
of the Society of St Paul who proclaim the Gospel
through the media of social communication.

*"The priest will not understand the greatness of
his office until he is in Heaven.
If he understood it on earth, he would die,
not of fear, but of love…*

*The priest is not a priest for himself;
he does not give himself absolution, he does not
administer the Sacraments to himself.
He is not for himself, he is for you."*

St John Vianney

PREFACE

"You renew the Church in every age by raising up men and women outstanding in holiness, living witnesses of your unchanging love." (Roman Missal, Second Preface of Holy Men and Women.)

As has often been said, the saints are gloriously different from each other; it is sin that is monotonous. One of the ways in which they are different is the effect they have on the Church, both in their own lifetime and later. Some saints were virtually unknown while they lived; others achieved honour quickly but were soon all but forgotten. The Curé of Ars belongs to that small group who were both celebrated in their own day, and whose significance only deepens with time.

Almost all books on the Curé leave one unsatisfied. Many are simply outdated, while others seem to be more a vehicle for the author's own whims. The only answer is to read for oneself what he said, but that is hard because he wrote nothing extensive and the only way to present his thought is to collect his short sayings under various headings.

But what a rich mine these sayings are! His teachings on the happiness of the Christian life, the Holy Spirit, Our Lady and the priesthood, to single out just a few, have such a glorious vitality and freshness, that it is a crime they are not better known.

Joanna Bogle's new book on the Curé is a timely and welcome contribution towards our rediscovery of the Curé as we respond to Pope Benedict's prophetic call for a "Year of the Priesthood". Its greatest value, however, will be to point readers to what the Curé himself said, which, as Joanna Bogle shows, he first lived in an exemplary way in his parish.

Mgr Keith Barltrop

CHAPTER ONE

*"In the morning, we should behave towards God
like an infant in its cradle.
As soon as it opens its eyes, it looks
quickly through the room to see its mother.
When it sees her, it begins to smile.
When it cannot see her, it cries."*[1]

~~~

The Church honours a vast variety of people as saints: heroes and martyrs, mystics, teachers, missionaries, founders of great religious orders, crusaders who helped the poor and downtrodden, and defenders of truth and justice in times of tyranny and oppression. But there is – so far, at any rate – only one saint who was simply a parish priest and that is John Vianney.

He is a well known saint. At the end of the nineteenth century and the beginning of the twentieth he was, along with St Thérèse of Lisieux and St Bernadette of Lourdes, a sort of emblem of a revived French Catholicism which had appeared to triumph over atheism and revolution, ushering in a new era.

The story of his life has already become the stuff of legend – the struggles to be ordained after many set-backs, the challenge of a bleak and apparently godless rural parish, the spiritual battles, the heroic fasting and dedication to prayer.

The problem with such a tale is that John Vianney

can seem a remote figure, a priest popularised by statues and pictures, who so rapidly acquired cult status that he never seems quite real, a character from a vanished world who has nothing to say to us now. So, while recognising that he lived in an age before motorways, mobile phones or the Internet, and in a rural France of bonnets and home-baking, where the fastest news arrived at the speed of a galloping horse, we can still reach him across the centuries and recognise in his life something with a profoundly practical message for today.

John Vianney was brought up in a country that was undergoing a turmoil horribly similar to those that would be experienced by many in the twentieth century. France in the first period of its revolution was a place of fear and horror – so much so that "The Terror" is the name that has been given to these months. Before excited crowds in the streets of the capital city, tumbrels brought people to be executed – by the newly-invented guillotine which sliced off heads with a speedy efficiency. Such executions seemed to combine the age-old excitement of war with the modernity of new machinery: a ghastly combination which was to echo and re-echo in years to come in different parts of Europe, with Nazi gas ovens and Stalinist gulags.

In 1786 when the baby Jean-Marie Vianney was born on May 8th in the village of Dardilly, in the region of Lyons, the French Revolution was three years off. As a tiny child, he would have been unaware of events, but by the 1790s, when the Church was plunged into the heart of things by the requirement of the new Civil Constitution of the Clergy, he would have started to hear the grown-ups talking of what was occurring – and in 1793, when the savage war in the Vendée had brought the deaths of huge numbers of men, women and children by the revolutionary armies, and some 40,000 people across France had been guillotined, every ordinary French family was living with fear.

This was civil war – with terror, oppression and misery marching alongside revolutionary slogans. Officially, historians list The Terror in France as raging from September 1793 to July 1794. French people were told that even the date itself was subject to change: 1794 was "Year 2" of the Republic, and the month of July was "Thermidor". The week was no longer to be of seven days but of ten: seven was an ugly and "uneven" number as well as having Christian connotations, being linked to the seven days of creation mentioned in Genesis and the Seven Sacraments of the Church. Ten was even, modern, and tidy.

Those not caught up in the drama of howling city mobs shouting at an execution, or passionate rural enclaves fighting back in the woods and hills, lived daily with hardship and fear. There was war with other European countries now, the British fleet seeking battle with France as refugees fleeing the terror brought news to London. War brought its own misery – it meant death and wounds, men conscripted into armies, farming and other crucial work disrupted, shortages of food and essentials.

People's deepest lives – their faith, the Christianity which had shaped France's history – was also caught up in all of this. The Church's bishops and senior clergy had for many years been seen as part of the nation's ruling structures; as these structures were replaced with new ones they were told to accommodate themselves, and many did. To swear allegiance to the new regime meant the possibility of living in reasonable comfort and continuing to ignore the ignorance, poverty, and neglect that flourished among many ordinary Catholics in France. Those clergy who chose a tougher path found themselves ministering in difficult circumstances, not dissimilar to those of Catholics in Elizabethan England a couple of centuries earlier, where it was necessary to celebrate Mass and the Sacraments in privacy, the devout gathering for the purpose in a safe house in a remote district.

The Vianneys were a devout family. When the local priest was replaced by one loyal to the new regime, they ceased attending the church and went secretly to Mass celebrated by priests they knew and trusted who had not taken the Civil oath. Such priests were courageous – the punishment for refusing to serve under the new Oath were severe. The guillotine was waiting. To be seen as counter-revolutionary was to court death.

The Vianneys were not alone in shunning the priests who had sworn allegiance to the State: although nothing had changed in the outward forms of the Mass, celebrated in Latin with vestments and incense, there was a recognition that something important was at stake here. The loyalty of the priest to the Church and to Christ mattered, and by taking the new oath he had compromised these. To be a true Catholic meant to belong to a universal Church loyal to St Peter's successor in Rome, and not one with a primary loyalty to a new government with a secularising agenda. Large numbers of faithful Catholics quietly found their way to Masses celebrated by priests in private houses.

Family life was the centre and core of community life. Families such as the Vianneys said prayers together at night. They worked together, and ate together. Children expected to learn skills from their parents. They expected to share in household tasks. They expected to share songs and games, jokes and traditions that had been passed down in the family and neighbourhood for centuries.

This was how the young John Vianney lived – with a deep sense of passed-on culture and wisdom, knowledge and skills, and a recognition that he was living in turbulent revolutionary times but was being taught timeless truths. His was a happy home – he would later always speak of his family with deep affection and love and teach with conviction about family duties and responsibilities.

It is rather difficult for us now to grasp how a rural family lived in Europe at that time. It was a way of living that was normal right up to a few decades ago, not in its practical day-to-day activities which of course changed with industrialisation, but in its economic and human inter-dependency and its sense of naturalness.

John Vianney grew up in a family home where not only the surname was shared but also faith, food, work, shelter, games, ideas, songs, celebrations, fears and fun. The Christian calendar chimed with the seasons of the year and Christian traditions named the foods and celebrations enjoyed on different occasions. Home was the primary source of medical care, information, and entertainment – and these were shared in turn with neighbours, friends and visitors.

The head of the Vianney family was John's grandfather Pierre and there were three generations living on the farm. Life was busy. Children and adults alike contributed to keeping things going. There were animals to be fed and tended – and in due course taken to market or slaughtered at home – crops and gardens yielding food, things to make and mend. Clothes were made at home, from wool produced from local sheep and spun and knitted in the house. Night prayers brought together a family that had been working as a team at various tasks around the house and land all day – and united them with dead relatives for whom they prayed regularly.

Needs of all kinds were brought before God, blessing sought on new projects and ventures. When a priest could be found, forgiveness and absolution were sought in the Sacrament of Penance, and Holy Communion received at Mass.

Who were these priests? Two were working in the area where the Vianneys lived: Fr Groboz, and Fr Charles Balley. When John was eleven years old and ready for his first confession, it was to Fr Groboz that he made it, kneeling, as he would later fondly recall, by the tall clock in the family house. Father Groboz worked as a cook, and maintained contact with his flock by systematic visiting, as the village church had become, temporarily, an alien place where the devout did not gather any more. Father Balley, who would eventually return there as parish priest, meanwhile worked as a carpenter while ministering to the spiritual needs of local families.

At the age of 15, John Vianney received his First Communion, with a group of other local young people gathered for the purpose at a family home, with the curtains drawn so that the activity was safe from prying eyes. Mass was said while the local farmers stayed outside, keeping watch, making sure that no stranger turned up unexpectedly. Officialdom was unable to penetrate the networks of such strong local loyalties.

A priest who brought Holy Communion to young people in such circumstances was a hero: a man who lived with a certain faith in the face of uncertainty and danger. All his life, John Vianney would have this understanding of the priesthood: it is not something connected with power and the importance of the State, it is not about prestige or a comfortable life. It is about getting people to Heaven by teaching them the truth about why we are all born, bringing them God's forgiveness through the Sacrament of Penance and feeding them with the Bread of Life in Holy Communion. This was something that he received, along with the Blessed Sacrament itself, from the priest before whom he knelt as a teenager in a farmhouse surrounded by people of his own family and neighbourhood who shared a common faith and culture.

The Vianney family were not unusual in being Catholics with a strong sense of traditional loyalty to the Church – the indication seems to be that their attitude towards the "nationalised" Church with its official clergy was fairly typical of farming families of their sort. The loyalty, however, was not a mere tribal thing but something centred on a deep love of God and a faith that was taught to their children with all the means at their disposal and in an atmosphere of family unity and affection. John grew up with a clear understanding of the faith and a desire to live it and communicate it.

If the Vianneys were unusual, it was perhaps in the welcome they gave to vagrants and strangers. It was known that they would feed tramps and passing travellers. From all accounts, there were many who benefited from this kindness, but there is one whose stay with the family would later be seen as hugely significant.

This was Benedict Labré, and his visit must have occurred a few years before John Vianney's birth, as Labre died in 1783. It would therefore have been something that would have been told to the young John as a notable piece of family history, something to be cherished and passed on.

The story of Benedict Labré is an extraordinary one. Born into a prosperous family, he longed to be a monk, with a deep conviction that he was called to do penance for sin. He tried in turn several religious orders including the Trappists, Carthusians and Cistercians, but all turned him down as he seemed mentally unstable. He was passionate about doing penance and sought to lead the simplest and most austere life possible, in a state of permanent pilgrimage to God. Eventually, he did this quite literally, taking to the road and owning nothing, wearing one simple shabby robe and sleeping out of doors or in the corner of a room if he was offered shelter. He walked this way to Rome and to various shrines, accepting abuse when his smelly arrival meant that he spoilt some family's pleasant evening and gratefully accepting food or shelter when it was offered. Devout, cheerful, friendly and holy, he befriended other homeless people and showed them that they too were loved and needed. Miracles became associated with him, including the multiplication of bread when only a small quantity had initially been donated by a well-wisher.

The arrival of Labré at the Vianney household would have been greeted in the same way as that of any other hungry traveller – he was welcomed and given food, shown friendly hospitality and invited to stay if needed. Probably his identity was not known at first but would have emerged during conversation. He had visited, on foot, the shrines at Paray-le-Monial and Compostella, among other places, and his final journey took him to Rome where he slept in the ruins of the Coliseum.

The Labré visit clearly remained strong in the family memory and was discussed many times as John was growing up. Patron saint of all tramps and beggars, of those with mental illness and those who feel outcasts from society, Labré was beatified in 1859. To have given shelter to someone widely known as a saint would be something that a Catholic family would discuss again and again, passing on every small detail of the memory so that it would not be forgotten.

In his work as a priest, John Vianney made frequently repeated calls for family holiness, for prayer together, and for the honouring of Catholic beliefs and values in the home. He was speaking from the heart and knew about it all from his own experience: even in difficult times, families can and must pass on the Faith, ensuring that children are taught how to pray and encouraged to know the love of God in the family circle. Sunday should be honoured as a day of rest – even if some new Government has tried to impose a ten-day week! – and the family home should be a place where virtues such as modesty, generosity, neighbourliness and care for the poor are taught and lived.

Even as a small boy, John Vianney knew that it required courage to live as a Catholic, but that there was great joy in the simple values of the Christian life and that people could help one another in their practical and spiritual needs. It was not necessary to give up on Christian living when things became difficult. But ordinary faithful people did need strong priests, and to be such a priest would surely be a glorious calling, something to which a man would have to respond with love and heroism.

NOTES

1. Catechetical Illustrations from nature. *Thoughts of the Curé d'Ars*, TAN Books USA.

CHAPTER TWO

*"We complain when we suffer.
We have much more reason to complain when
we do not suffer, since nothing so likens us to
Our Lord as the bearing of His Cross."*[1]

~ ~ ~

There is no doubt that John Vianney knew from a young age that he felt called to the priesthood and he probably knew that it would be a call that would be strongly tested. How would a country boy, at a particularly difficult time for the Church in France, get the opportunity to study in a seminary and be ordained? From where would funds come for his education?

Things moved slowly. The first person John would approach about the priesthood was, naturally, his father. Mathieu Vianney was a devout man whose love for the Church was very great, but he had a large family to support and needed his son's help on the farm. Times were difficult and all hands were needed to keep things going and ensure food for the family.

John also approached his parish priest, Fr Charles Balley – the local hero who had ministered to people during the worst days of the Terror and who was much loved. John would later recall that it was in the year 1804 that he first spoke to his father and to Fr Balley about his longing to be a priest. Father Balley encouraged him and helped to make the necessary enquiries and arrangements but, with family obligations on the farm, it would be a further two years before he could be spared to go to the seminary and begin his studies.

Things were now improving for the Church in France. This was now the post-revolutionary era; Napoleon had arrived on the scene. In 1802 a Concordat between France and the Papacy enabled a new chapter to open. For his part, the Pope – Pius VII – had to recognise the legitimate role of the state, while Napoleon made a formal acknowledge of Papal authority. In 1804 the Emperor Napoleon crowned himself, insisting on the Pope being present at the ceremony. A rapprochement of sorts was achieved between the faithful Catholics of France and the rulers of the nation. The days of the Terror had given way to new realities. It was going to be possible for normal parish life to return to the village churches, and for priests to minister to the people as had been done for generations.

The Church had to some extent been purified by the events of the Terror. Catholics had seen the heroism of martyrs – men and women had been guillotined, tied to rafts on the Loire and drowned, or kept in filthy prisons until they died of cold and hunger. The suffering had been horrific. France had been presented with a vision of the Church not as an institution associated with a any sort of privilege but as something rather different, and noble under intense persecution: "Stripped of wealth and power, the Church in France now concentrated on her fundamental mission to preach the Gospel and serve the people in fidelity to Apostolic teaching. There was a return to the traditional Catholic values and an intellectual appreciation of the Church as the 'Mother of art and Guardian of patriotism'."[2]

It was in this atmosphere and with a sense of great dedication that John Vianney began classes with Fr Balley.

Popular history has subsequently painted a picture of John Vianney as a man of limited intellectual abilities, whose struggles at the seminary were due to ignorance and even stupidity. This is inaccurate. He thought and spoke of himself as someone slow and dim-witted, but in reality was a brilliant and gifted man who delighted in extensive reading, studied with care and diligence, and showed every evidence of considerable learning in a wide range of subjects. His problem, on arrival at Fr Balley's seminary, was simply that he had received little formal education and had absolutely no knowledge of Latin, then the standard language in which much study was done. He was now twenty years old and had spent most of his life in outdoor work. The only way he could acquire proficiency in Latin was to join the junior class and sit with twelve-year-olds.

There is a story about one of John's fellow-pupils, Mathias Loras, punching him on the head when Vianney was unable to answer a question. Confessing to his own stupidity, John knelt before him in humility. The boy wept, and never forgot the incident. Years later, as a missionary bishop in America, he would recall every detail of the event and often spoke of it. (Loras, whose father and older brother had both been killed in the Terror, would give years of service to the emerging Church in America, founding schools for Indians and becoming, in 1837, the first Bishop of Dubuque, Iowa.[3])

John Vianney, struggling with Latin, a grown man sitting at a school desk in a room of youngsters almost half his age, was already living an austere life. He fasted – years later he would say that he had done so imprudently, eating nothing sometimes for a week at a time in an effort to engage his brain solely on academic work – and he also spent long hours in prayer. He was utterly dedicated to the goal of ordination, but it seemed very hard to attain.

At one point, John's failure at lessons seemed so total that he told Fr Balley that perhaps he should give up and go home where he could at least be useful on the farm. But Fr Balley encouraged him. He suggested a pilgrimage to a shrine: the shrine of St Francis Regis in southern France. John walked all the way there, begging his food on the way.

Saint Francis Regis, born in 1597, was a Jesuit of the counter-Reformation era, filled with zeal, who worked with plague victims in Toulouse, founded homes for destitute girls rescued from prostitution, and was a popular and effective preacher who reconciled many people who had left the Church.

Himself a gifted and intelligent man, well qualified in theology and philosophy, he was happy to work among the poor and uneducated, to whom he preached missions. He ignored hardships and dangers, walking long distances in all weathers, and eventually died of pneumonia. He was canonised in 1737 and his shrine became a popular place of pilgrimage.

At the shrine John Vianney prayed for just one thing – help with his lessons. On his return, he felt renewed. The students at the small seminary were now being confirmed, John among them. He took the name "Baptiste" as his Confirmation name, and from that date on – the year was 1807 – he added it to his own name.

He was now in his early twenties. Things had been delayed, but surely the path to priesthood was now open? No. A new problem presented itself. Napoleon was at war with half of Europe and he needed soldiers. Young men studying at the seminary were exempt but in 1809, due to an administrative mistake, John was called up for military duty.

What happened next was almost absurd. Ordered to join his regiment at Bayonne, he fell ill on the way and had to be taken to hospital, where he almost died. When he eventually recovered, he was given new orders and told to report to the authorities at Roanne. The morning his troop departed, he went to pray in the local church – and when he returned to the town square to join them, they had already vanished. Setting off on foot to find them, he became lost on the way. Eventually, he was befriended by a man who had deserted from the army. By now winter had set in and he took John off to his own home village of Les Robins, near Les Noës, in a forest district. Here, cut off in a remote district, John found shelter with the Fagot family, who were relatives of the Mayor. They gave him a new name, Jerome Vincent, in case the authorities arrived to ask any questions. Living as a member of the family, he worked around the house and farm, and also taught the village children how to read, establishing a small makeshift school.

It was while he was working there that news arrived of an amnesty for all defaulters and deserters from the Army. Napoleon had married and, as part of the celebrations for the wedding, he had made this announcement of national goodwill. The year was 1810. Once more John took to the road and made his way back to his own district. Finally, in 1812, he was able to enter the seminary at Varrieres, near Montbrison. He was now formally a student for the priesthood. The next stage would be to go to the main seminary of St Irenaeus at Lyons, but, while at Varrieres, his struggles to cope with Latin were still evident. He had had no opportunity to read or use the language for almost five years: what he had managed to learn earlier had almost vanished. The very formal style of teaching, with structured lessons to be absorbed by rote, was also something difficult for a man used to practical skills and the application of the mind in a mature way.

In fact, in his later years as a priest, John Vianney's farming skills, his years of outdoor work and his closeness to farming families, were to be part of his brilliance as a pastor. He used practical allusions to everyday rural life in his sermons. He understood the hardships and challenges of the lives of country people and he spoke to them as one of their own. But in these college years his lack of easy familiarity with the accepted academic style of the day was a handicap to be overcome and a source of anxiety and grief to him.

Father Balley, his mentor and friend, came to his rescue when, on entering the major seminary, John did so badly in the theology examination that he was told it was impossible for him to remain. All seemed hopeless. It is reported that, on leaving the seminary he went back to his own home village, stood by his mother's grave and wept, begging the help of her prayers.[4] Father Balley interceded for him with the seminary professors and he was given an extra chance. After months of further tuition, he took the examination again, to no avail. Recognising that the problem was purely one of a difficulty with written examinations, Fr Balley begged that he might be re-examined orally, and in French, back at Ecully in familiar surroundings. This time he not only passed but did extremely well. The examiners noted something that could not be apparent from the candidate's unskilled writing: he was unusually devout, knew Church doctrine because he loved it and lived it and could explain it with quite unusual clarity and understanding.

John was ordained deacon in the June of 1815. It was an extraordinary time. Napoleon had been defeated at Waterloo. The countryside was swarming with foreign troops. No one knew what would happen next and who would rule France after Napoleon's downfall. In the chaos of these days John had to walk the eighty miles from Ecully to Grenoble where his ordination to the priesthood would take place. The Austrian troops and the long journey were the final hurdles to be overcome. On 13 August 1815, in the seminary at Grenoble, John Vianney was ordained a priest.

NOTES

1. *Thoughts of the Curé d'Ars*, Burns and Oates 1967, Tan Books 1984.
2. *John Vianney, The Life and Times of the Curé of Ars*, J.B. Midgley, CTS 2008.
3. Pierre-Jean Mathias Loras, born 1792. at Lyons. In the diocese of Dubuque, where he arrived in 1839, he was responsible for building a number of churches, serving the immigrants from France, Germany and Ireland, and died in 1858. Loras Boulevard in Dubuque is named after him.
4. *The Curé d'Ars Today*, Father George Rutler, Ignatius Press, San Francisco, 1988.

CHAPTER THREE

*"There is no one who cannot pray –
and pray at all times and in all places;
by night or day, when hard at work or resting,
in the country, at home, or when travelling."*[1]

~~~

After the struggle to be ordained, John Vianney began his pastoral work with the best possible mentor – he was appointed as assistant to Fr Balley and went to work alongside him in the parish of Ecully. Under Fr Balley's guidance, he continued to study theology, and every day he learned more and more about how to be a good priest.

Who was Fr Balley? In John's boyhood he had been the staunchly loyal priest of the district, around whom faithful Catholics gathered, attending Mass and receiving the Sacraments and ignoring the usurper in the parish church whom they saw as nothing more than an appointee of the revolutionary government. Father Balley's life was one of hardship and difficulty – travelling to remote farms to celebrate Mass, enduring hunger and cold, and not knowing for how long it would be necessary to minister to people in this way.

Now fully restored to his parish, Fr Balley worked hard as he had always done. His was a life of penance. He wore a hair-shirt, and fasted almost continuously, relying for nourishment on boiled potatoes, often of dubious quality and age. His academic qualifications were such that he had been offered a full-time post at the seminary, but he had declined this as he saw his primary duty as being towards his parishioners. His store of theological knowledge – especially pastoral theology, and the practical applications of Christian teachings to everyday life – was at the service of his new young curate, who was an eager pupil.

Living in great simplicity, with no luxuries at all, Fr Balley set an example of austerity which matched what John Vianney had already mapped out as being the way a priest should live. Local people used to smile to see them setting out, in atrocious weather, to visit the shrine of Our Lady of Fourvière, sharing one shabby umbrella.

Inflicting serious penances on himself, and spending long hours in prayer, Fr Balley was radiant in his priesthood and very much loved by local people. For John Vianney, he was the model of priesthood around which his own understanding formed and took practical shape: this was how a priest should be, how he should live, how he should pray.

In 1817 Fr Balley became very ill and it was clear he was dying. His curate was with him in his last days, heard his last confession, and prayed with him as he died. For the rest of John Vianney's life, he would cherish the old umbrella they had shared together, and also the old cracked shaving mirror that Fr Balley had used "because it had reflected the good priest's face". In due course these two items would come to be carefully cherished by others too, associated with not just one but two saintly priests and eventually finding their way into a mueum at Ars.

John stayed on at Ecully as a new parish priest was appointed. This one, Fr Tripier, was very different from Fr Balley and worked in a very different way. He saw the clergy as having a certain social status locally and wanted to know why his young curate did not attend some of the smarter functions. When John made the excuse that his one cassock was too shabby for grand occasions, the parish priest asked why he didn't have another.

The Vicar-General of the diocese was, at this time, making new appointments. The small hamlet of Ars was without a priest. It consisted of only a few scattered dwellings, in a rather bleak area, and its people were not likely to be impressed by the clergy – one former parish priest had renounced his orders and now ran a shop, another had arrived with a serious illness and died after less than a month.

The journey to Ars from Ecully would be accomplished on foot. John needed to take only essentials – books and a bedstead. These would go in a handcart. John was used to walking. Thin and lean, he walked with a steady pace in his shabby black cassock, with his tricorne hat, standard headgear for priests at that time, usually tucked under his arm.

His approach to Ars has become legendary. Some children were playing as he stopped to ask the way.

One boy volunteered to show him the route and his new parish priest set the tone for the future right away: "You have shown me the way to Ars, and I will show you the way to Heaven". Nothing else mattered. The task of John Vianney, parish priest of Ars, was to get its people where they belonged at the end of their earthly lives – with God in the Paradise won for them on the Cross.

A statue of the priest and the boy now marks the spot, but there was no landmark or signpost of any kind when John Vianney first passed along the road with his handcart. It was a damp and misty day. The church at Ars had lost its tower in the Revolution, when rioters tore it down and used the building for meetings of a club of atheists. Local people had learned to keep quiet about their faith during those years, but had never completely lost it. Since then, they had become largely indifferent. They were not opposed to the new priest, or rude to him, but had become used to being wary and cynical. Priests who had arrived in recent years had not stayed. There had been no systematic teaching of the truths of the Faith. The church was a tradition, a link with all that had gone before and was an immoveable part of life – but not a part that spoke to the heart or challenged the soul.

John Vianney's installation as Parish Priest took place on 13 February 1818, in a ceremony during which he was led from the small presbytery to the door of the church and presented with his stole, which was placed around his neck, signifying that he was now responsible for the souls of the people of Ars. They did not know it at the time, but he would make their small parish famous around the world, leading not just them and their families but hundreds and thousands of other people on the road towards heaven.

Because the story of the Curé of Ars is well known, a certain tradition has grown up around it, with a sort of ritual quality in its telling. The legend is that this was a very evil village, full of sin and almost wholly lacking in the things of God – and John Vianney arrived to put it right. This works well as a pious legend and has a truth in it that works for every parish where a good and holy priest starts putting people at peace with God, but was Ars really a hotbed of sin?

Ars was an ordinary corner of rural France, where ordinary evil abounded. It flourished in particular because the Revolution and its aftermath had helped to ensure that the things which banish evil – the Mass, the Sacraments, repentance, God's mercy, prayer – had been absent or pushed to the margins. People knew about God, they knew why there was a Church, they knew their need of it, but everything had become muddled and confused and there was a general feeling that perhaps these things didn't matter as much as they had done at one time.

Because they had not been taught the Faith for a long time and because life seemed meaningless and without purpose, with God as a mere traditional accessory stitched on at the edge of things, people sought pleasure and meaning where they could. The local pubs saw sessions of what today we would probably call "binge-drinking". Family life lacked the dimension of prayer. There was a sordid side to village social life.

The new Curé did not have to introduce the idea of God. He was speaking to people who had a strong heritage of faith and whose lives were steeped in Catholic tradition. Since time immemorial, every child born in the village had been baptised. The church was the only place where people could marry, and the place where all funerals were held. The framework of the Church's seasons marked out the year, saints' names were automatically given to children, everyone knew what a priest was and what he represented. But the problem was that for many years there had not been a priest who truly cared for people's souls, or who was a man from an ordinary country farming family who truly identified with the village people and could speak to them in a way they understood. It had more or less come to be accepted that a priest was someone different – a man of learning, perhaps, or with some social status, or simply someone who found the everyday realities of a farming community too sordid and brutal and was tempted to retreat to his books and the company of more refined or intellectual companions.

The new Curé was something quite different. It

is really quite extraordinary: he presented the people of Ars with a message which would utterly change their lives and he did so in a way that was not even, initially, very attractive.

At first his congregations were small. Adults and children alike were often at work on Sundays. This was a farming community, always at the mercy of the weather, and livelihoods depended on seizing a crucial day to get crops sown or reaped – a sunny morning spent at Mass looked like a dreadful error if the next day brought a storm which wrecked crops that could by then have been safely gathered and stored away.

Initially, he wrote out all his sermons laboriously, using a standard manual that had been produced some years earlier. He then read the resulting work aloud. This made the style formal, and the message – which was always very stern – presented in extremely rigid terms. He also raised his voice and spoke very forcefully. But later he abandoned the lengthy written essays, and spoke in a more natural way.

He spoke about Heaven, Hell and sin, about the reason for human existence and the love that God has for everyone. He spoke with severity about the absolute necessity of keeping Sunday as a day of rest – attendance at Mass as the priority, of course, followed by no work, no trade or business of any kind and no activity that could even be deemed as connected with these things. He also spoke, repeatedly and in a very detailed way, about the evils of dancing.

Because much of what he said rings oddly today, it is worth looking at some of this in greater detail, but it must first be established that his message was centred on the message that human beings have been made by God and are destined for eternity. What really matters in life is that each should live in such a way as to avoid eternal punishment. As parish priest, his job was to bring people to God and save them from the horror of an eternity spent in the punishment reserved for those who broke God's laws and commandments. Absolutely nothing else mattered as much as this and he saw it as folly to pretend otherwise.

He did not need to speak, as a priest would have to do today, about the reality of God as such – country people in France in the early nineteenth century knew that God existed. What he had to do was bring the message of Christ alive, so that it really made sense and was not merely a tradition. To be a Christian, he explained, is a joyful thing, but it involves a daily struggle against evil and a daily need to live in the presence of God.

"Never forget that it is at the beginning of each day that God has the necessary grace for the day ready for us. He knows exactly what opportunities we shall have to sin… and will give us everything we need if we ask him then. That is why the devil does all he can to prevent us from our Morning Prayers, or to make us say them badly."

Above all, he directed people to Christ in the

Eucharist, present in the Tabernacle and ready to be welcomed into human hearts and souls in Holy Communion. He wanted people to know and love Christ in a deep and personal way, to be close to him, to pray often, to be on warm and affectionate terms with him, to respond with joy to the great love that Christ gave them.

From the beginning of his time at Ars, the confessional was to be a central point of his ministry. He urged people not to delay, but to hurry to the Sacrament of Penance, where "God makes greater speed to pardon a penitent sinner than a mother to snatch her child out of the fire."

As his style changed, Fr Vianney used images from everyday life, from the countryside and the working lives of the people. He spoke about ordinary sins: things like sloth and greed, envy, gossiping and the neglect of prayer.

"We must be like shepherds in the fields during the winter. They have a fire, but from time to time they search about for sticks to keep it alive. If we knew how to keep up the fire of love of God in our hearts by prayers and good works, it would not go out."

"If we are tempted to thoughts of envy against our neighbour, far from letting him see it by our cold manner, we must go out of our way to be friendly, and do him any service that lies in our power."

"How many moments can be lost in doing nothing, or in doing wrong, or in listening to the suggestions of the devil, or in obeying him!"

He was emphatic in his denouncing of sin, using language that we would today find unfashionable. But he spoke bluntly, because his aim was to get people to Heaven, and there was no time to waste.

"Christ wept over Jerusalem… I weep over you. How can I help weeping, my brethren? Hell exists. It is not my invention. God has told us. And you pay no heed… you do all that is necessary to be sent there. You blaspheme the name of God. You spend your evenings in the cabarets. You give yourselves to the sinful pleasures of dancing. You steal from your neighbour's field. You do a world of things that are offences against God. Do you think, then, that God does not see you? He sees you, my children, as I see you and you will be treated accordingly. What misery! Hell exists. I implore: think of Hell. Do you think your Curé will let you be cast into Hell to burn there for ever and ever? Are you going to cause this suffering to your Curé?"[2]

While so much of what St John Vianney said rings true today, especially the warnings about Hell, sin and the importance of a regular life of prayer, there are details which do sound odd. Chief of these concerns dancing. It does need to be said that there were gatherings where the drinking and dancing sometimes made for sordid spectacles. He wanted people to be realistic about occasions of sin. But he went much further than this, insisting that it was sinful to engage in any sort of dancing, at any time.

He persuaded the family at the manor house, where occasional formal receptions had sometimes included very sedate dancing, that even this was wrong and must be stopped. In the confessional he refused absolution to anyone who attended a dance, even to watch. Village gatherings where young people had danced out in the square by the church to the sound of violins on feast-days, were to be stopped – on one occasion he paid a violinist to go away and he preached so often and so vigorously against all forms of dancing that eventually all attempts to arrange such events petered out. He refused absolution to anyone who admitted having attended a dance, unless a firm promise was made never to attend again.[3]

He also preached about modesty of dress for women – which seems to us odd in a time and place where women's clothes covered them from neck to toe, shoulder to wrist, even in the hottest weather. For the women on the farms around Ars, there was little or no opportunity to add lace or delicate embroidery to the simple made-to-last garments in their modest wardrobes – much less to obtain the crinolines or other fashions that people wore in towns or cities. On one occasion when he visited a family, one of the daughters was sewing a linen collar with some small decoration and he offered to buy it from her for a few pence, saying that he would give it to a dog. He had a horror of anything that seemed to indicate luxuries or vanity.

The problem with all of this is that we see it from

the perspective of a very different world. Fashions have changed beyond all recognition. Today, it is standard for most young women to dress in the blue denim trousers which, back in nineteenth-century France were standard workmen's wear and would only have been forced on a woman as an absolute humiliation. Such garments, if worn at church by a young mother, would probably have been seen as a form of public penance or punishment. Today Catholic shops at places of pilgrimage sell, for the pious, mantillas of delicate black lace of a type that would have been regarded as highly sensuous and immoral in an era when the rule for women was heavy bonnets framing the face, covering the hair and free of anything like black lace which might have sent out a very flighty image. We simply cannot always think ourselves back into a vanished age.

Perhaps St John Vianney knew his own people, and a message that would get them to Heaven. He was a man of his time and preached using the training he had been given. In fairness it could also be added that some of his sermons on related subjects also strike a note of practical realism: he spoke about the evils of not giving adequate privacy for dressing and undressing, of the importance of having babies and children properly dressed so that they would not wander around naked, and called for dignity and decency in family life.

But in his war on sin, the Curé did not just preach, and he did not just hear confessions. He undertook penances. The people of Ars were his children, and like a good Father he wanted the best for them. He wanted them to go to Heaven. He did not want a single one to be lost. He explained to them patiently that Heaven and Hell were real, that at death Eternity waited. Where would they go? It was his task as their spiritual father, as their Curé, to lead them to God, and to thwart the Devil of his prey.

John Vianney had long lived with a regime of fasting and prayer and now he renewed this with greater intensity. The people for whom he prayed were those entrusted to him by God. What a huge responsibility! The only things that mattered was their souls. In seeking the good, in following God, they would also lead happier and better lives while still here on earth. Jealousy and drunkenness, immorality and laziness, meant misery as well as sin. No one benefited but the devil.

So the Curé must take responsibility, and make up in his own life any penance that was lacking in theirs. He slept on a hard bed, with no mattress and no pillow – a block of wood sufficed. Food was minimal and consisted chiefly of potatoes eaten once a day, with sometimes a glass of milk. Gradually he developed a routine of cooking potatoes at the start of each week, and simply eating a couple (cold) every day, even though by the end of the week they were inevitably mouldy. Always clean and neat, he wore just the same old shabby cassock every day, and beneath it a spiked bracelet on one arm, and a hair shirt.

At first, the congregation for Masses at Ars was small. People came out of curiosity to see the new priest, or because there was nothing much else to do. But they stayed, and the numbers grew. It was not that the sermons made the listeners comfortable – quite the contrary. They learned that death and judgement were real things and that Satan wanted to greet them in Hell for an eternity of suffering. The way to avoid this was to obey God's Commandments, to avoid sin and to repent fervently after sinning and seek absolution, and to pray often and with great devotion.

If the sermons were severe, they were preached with such obvious sincerity and devotion that it was impossible not to be moved and touched. This was a priest who was serious about the truths he taught: he wanted to save the people from an eternity of misery and punishment.

"The word salvation is one of those used most frequently by the Curé d'Ars. What does it mean for him? To be saved is to be delivered from the sin that separates from God, dries up the heart, and risks eternal separation from the love of God – which would be the worst unhappiness of all. To be saved is to live united to God, to see God. To be saved is likewise to be reintroduced into a true communion with others, because our sins very often consist in wounding the love of neighbour, justice, truth, the respect for his goods and his body: all this is contrary to the will of God."[4]

The Curé was able to explain things in a simple, straightforward way that people could understand. He came from a country family and had grown up on a farm, knowing hard work and family solidarity, the rhythm of the seasons and the importance of everyday duties and responsibilities.

"The commandments of God" he told them "are the guides which God gives us to show us the road to Heaven; like the names written on street corners, to point the way."

NOTES

1. *Thoughts of the Curé d'Ars,* TAN Books USA.
2. Quoted in *The Curé of Ars Today* by George William Rutler, Ignatius Press, 1988.
3. For a fuller examination of this, see Lancelot C. Sheppard *The Curé d'Ars, portrait of a parish priest,* London, 1958.
4. Pope John Paul II, retreat given at Ars, October 1986.

CHAPTER FOUR

*Rarely has a pastor been so acutely aware
of his responsibilities, so consumed by a desire to
wrest his people from the sins of their luke-warmness.*[1]

~~~

The people of Ars came to know that their parish priest loved them. He worked tirelessly at his parish duties. When he visited local families, he was cheerful and kind. He would accept a glass of wine offered in someone's home because it would have been rude and hurtful to refuse. But it was known that he ate almost nothing, and gave away any small luxury that came his way. He had given his mattress and pillow to a poor man who had neither. If he was given new clothes he promptly gave them away and continued to wear his old worn cassock.

Initially, he had a housekeeper, a pious woman of the village known as Mother Bibost, who cooked and cleaned. But it became clear that she had very little to do, since he would not eat ordinary meals, only his simple potatoes and he had given away most of the furniture. It was Mére Bibost who first began to notice his very strict penances and to mention them to others. It became clear that, as he simply did not eat ordinary meals, he did not need a housekeeper and so he sent her away and she returned to other work in the village.

He spent money only on the things that mattered – including good vestments and altar-cloths for the church, replacing those that were shabby and grimy. Gradually, he made the little church more beautiful and people came to understand it as the most important place in the village, the place where God welcomed everyone. Over the years it would be considerably extended, with extra side-chapels which involved major work creating extensions to the building on either side. One chapel was dedicated to St John the Baptist, with an inscription reminding visitors that he had died because of a dance.

His insistence on the importance of family prayers in the evening led him to gather people in church for this purpose – many families found it difficult to lead their own prayers at home, but it felt all right to do it as a group. He organised glorious processions and celebrations for the great feasts of the Church's year, arranging costumes for the small children and bringing everyone together with a sense of doing something beautiful for God.

His severe penances meant that he looked thin, with hollow cheeks. In addition to the hair shirt, the loss of sleep and the minimal food, he scourged himself with knotted cords. But he was always joyful, and pleasant in company. Children enjoyed his visits to their homes. He talked about the things of God to anyone and everyone, fitting in easily and naturally to any circle. He understood about hard work, and talked a language everyone understood.

People started coming to confession in large numbers and he began to spend several hours each day in the confessional. It was impossible to keep things secret from him there. He knew when some one tried to fudge about, for example, the length of time since a previous confession, or omitted a serious sin or a series of sins.

Father John Vianney had not arrived to find himself friendless in Ars. On the contrary, the lady of the local manor house was glad to welcome him and had arranged for some furniture to be sent to the little presbytery to make it cosy. This he duly sent back – it did not fit with his ideas of penance – but he was on friendly terms with Mme Marie-Anne Colombe Garnier des Garets, from the start. The local people simply called her Mademoiselle d'Ars.

She liked to meet for prayer with like-minded people of her own sort, and did so regularly. They were, like many of the devout Catholics in France at that time, rather influenced by Jansenism – best described as a form of Catholic Puritanism – and Fr Vianney saw it as a crucial task to draw her gently out of this. She was in her sixties when Fr Vianney came to Ars, and was living in a simple style amid the slightly shabby grandeur of the chateau. She fulfilled her neighbourly duties well, helping local families when illness or poverty struck hard, and she led her little household in prayers every day. Her prayerful devotion to the Church was a great support to Fr Vianney. Over the years her brother, living in

Paris, would send items that were needed for the church, including statues that were beautiful and of good quality, the sort of thing that the Curé wanted in order to help people lift their minds and hearts to God.

Mademoiselle d'Ars began to join other villagers in the church for evening prayers, rather than saying them at home in her own private chapel. She came to love and admire the Curé, as did her brother the Vicomte Francois des Garets, who met him for the first time in 1819 on a visit to the village. He "was captivated by the parish priest and dipped into his not inconsiderable purse on more than one occasion. In this way a canopy, a monstrance, an exposition throne, a black velvet chasuble with red orphreys for Good Friday, found their way to the little sacristy, though the people had to wait until 1826 before they saw the new canopy borne over the Blessed Sacrament through the village street at the Corpus Christi procession. When put together it was discovered to be too large to be carried through the church door and could not be used until the Vicomte had donated a new facade to the church and enlarged the doorway."[2]

Jansenism was something which infected many aspects of Catholic life and some commentators have noted that there are traces of it in John Vianney's style as well. But he also played a major role in helping to ensure its passing. Essentially, Jansenism, named after Cornelius Jansen, 1585-1638, emphasised human sin and unworthiness and an almost Calvinistic sense of the gap between man and God. It was opposed by the Jesuits who emphasised God's loving mercy and forgiveness, and by the cult of devotion to the Sacred Heart and the personal affection Christ feels for each individual person. But its influence lingered for years.

Books and sermons promoting a Jansenist view were influential in France, partly perhaps because the Revolution halted the promotion of alternative viewpoints and prevented the publication and dissemination of good materials. Condemned by the Church, the ideas in Jansenism were formally banned from being spread about, but in the nineteenth century they affected the thinking and preaching on topics concerning sin, human unworthiness and, especially, matters concerning sexual morality. In the training of priests, which had in any case been badly disrupted by the Revolution, "it seemed much easier to inculcate respect for authority and practise of the rule, rather than to light in their souls the fire of holiness… The professors in the seminaries or in the presbytery schools, survivors of the Revolution… could have been but poorly taught or had little education. Moreover, where were books to be got? The libraries had been sacked and the books stolen or auctioned off to the highest bidder, or even been sold by the pound like apples."[3]

Father John Vianney consistently spoke of God's love and mercy, and if his style in naming sins and emphasising the horrors of Hell has a very nineteenth-century and faintly Jansenistic style to it, this needs to be balanced against the reality of his commitment to the joyful truth that God loves to forgive and seeks to draw all souls to Heaven. In the confessional, Fr Vianney gave light penances to sincere penitents, saying that he would do the rest himself. Living what by any measure was a life of supreme hardship – little rest, minimal food, deliberate self-inflicted penances – he was nevertheless a serene and joyful person to whom others were always attracted. There was nothing sour or miserable about him.

He was also dedicated to the idea that people should receive Holy Communion frequently – ideally every Sunday at Mass – and this was considered absolutely revolutionary at the time. Following the Revolution with its horrors, the approach taken by the Church seems to have been that it was necessary to be extremely strict, to insist on people being made to understand their own unworthiness, and the terrible blasphemy involved in receiving Holy Communion while in a state of sin, and that in this strictness lay the only hope of the Church's survival in whatever situation might occur in the years ahead. In the training of priests, there was an emphasis on this. As a result, some people, especially the very scrupulous, did not go to Communion for years at a time. Father Vianney, in suggesting to his flock that they should receive Communion four times a year, had to struggle against deeply-held ideas. One author writes that "for the Curé of Ars… the Blessed Eucharist was to aid the Christian to acquire perfection, not crown it. Separating him from his time, we find in him the first fruits of the doctrine concerning frequent communion."[4]

There were plenty of things that needed attention in Ars. The children of the village attended school for only a very short time each year, because they were needed for work on the farms. They had not received systematic instruction in their religion for many years. Father Vianney thus organised classes – separately for boys and girls. These were held very early in the morning, so as not to interfere with the working day – and the first child to arrive received a holy picture, thus ensuring prompt attendance.

He looked to the longer term, and arranged for two local young women, Catherine Lassagne and Benedicta Lardet, to go to a college run by nuns at Fareins. Here, they would be trained as teachers and in due course return to the village to work. They would later be joined by Jeanne-Marie Chanay from the nearby village of Jassans who would assist with cooking and cleaning. The particular need was for a school for girls, and also an orphanage.

Using his own family money that had come to him on the death of his father, together with other donations, Fr Vianney created "La Providence" which was to be a school for girls and also, more importantly, a home for girls who were orphans, or whose families were unable to look after them. There were many of these in France at that time, their plight the result of the chaos produced by the Revolution and its aftermath.

"La Providence" began in a small house with just one large room downstairs and two above, but it soon had to be enlarged. The three women running it worked hard. "They received no salary and often there was hardly enough to eat; very soon they were overcrowded… Soon to the girls of the village were added those from neighbouring parishes; word had gone round that there was a good free school in Ars and parents hastened to take advantage of it."

"For three years the school progressed with day girls and boarders, and then Fr Vianney, who had been struck by the unhappy lot of many orphans in the district, sent away the boarders and transformed the institution into a combined orphanage and day school. Girls from the age of eight were received, sometimes homeless young women of sixteen or seventeen were accepted for a time; all were trained for farm work or housework, taught sewing and cooking. It was not long before they were in demand from the larger houses in the vicinity. If ever Fr Vianney encountered some unfortunate girl in the district he contrived to make room for her in his beloved Providence. At one time there were sixty crowded into the small building and though it had been enlarged when the orphanage was begun it was still hardly big enough for half that number…"[5]

The regular catechism classes given by the Curé were a central part of school life, as was the personal concern that he brought to the establishment's domestic needs. He was a practical man and trained from childhood to turn his hand to all sorts of tasks, so when the house needed extending he built walls and mended furniture with dedication and skill. With this example before them, people rallied to help at every stage.

The girls at La Providence wore the bulky long skirts and close-fitting tied-under-the-chin bonnets that were common among country women of the district at the time. Their education was centred on practical skills that would help them to earn their living when they left.

The catechism classes that Fr Vianney gave to the girls started to draw others. In the early years, before great crowds started to come to the village, it was a quiet and even cosy scene as the priest, who was much loved by the children, arrived in cassock and surplice to start the instruction. The three women running La Providence always sat with the girls, and usually sewed as they listened to the Curé. Sometimes chickens would wander in clucking. But then other people started to arrive, squeezing in at the back of the room, listening at the windows, gathering outside and straining to hear. The classes had to be taken to the parish church.

The people of the village began to speak of their parish priest as a saint. They would see him praying in the church at all hours, and they knew that he barely slept, and then sometimes on the floor. They saw how he laboured willingly at all sorts of practical tasks with a cheerful goodwill, but ate very little, gave away any small treat that came his way, and never simply relaxed in an armchair. They saw with what fervour he knelt in prayer, how genuinely he wept over their sins, and how simple and straightforward he was in speaking of God, and of God's love.

When he prayed, God answered. People began to speak of miracles. During one difficult period, there was not enough grain at "La Providence" to make bread to feed the little girls. Father Vianney took a statue of St Francis Regis – to whom he had prayed so hard in his student days – and placed it in the attic where the last small mound of grain was stored. He gathered the children and they all prayed together. A teacher went up in due course to get the grain – and on opening the door was met by a cascade of grain that poured out and down the stairs.

The children enjoyed their bread – and the whole village knew of the story, groups hurrying to see for themselves the great pile of grain, and to marvel at it. Father Vianney simply told them "The good God is very good!"

That was the first of many extraordinary things that, over the next months and years, would bring vast crowds to Ars. Father Vianney would not speak of these things, except to deflect attention to a saint whose cult he wanted to popularise – St Philomena.

Her name comes from the Greek ("one who loves God"), and is taken from a tomb found in the Roman catacombs, which at this time (early nineteenth century) were being explored and opened up in a new wave of interest in archaeology. The cult of this young Roman martyr from the early days of the Church had been popularised by visitors to Rome, including a devout French woman, Pauline Jaricot. The story appealed to the post-Revolutionary Church of France with its new sense of romantic and ardent spirituality.

The story of Pauline Jaricot is worth adding here. Born into a well-to-do Catholic family in 1799, she felt called at the end of her teens to dedicate her life wholly to God. Rather than entering a convent, she chose to remain at home, living as simple a lifestyle as possible and vowed to personal poverty. Inspired by a recognition that new explorations and forms of travel were opening up whole new continents to the Church, she wanted to help the foreign missions and conceived the idea of a "living rosary". It was launched among girls working as maids and servants in the big houses, and consisted of groups of ten, who met to pray the Rosary together and to collect, from each girl, just one sou (the tiniest possible coin, perhaps equivalent to our 1p). The money, faithfully recorded, was collected together and from this came the Society for the Propagation of the Faith, which over the years would fund the work of missionaries working in Africa, Asia, China and the Americas.

Pauline Jaricot was taken ill on a journey to Rome, in dramatic circumstances when crossing the Alps. She prayed for help to St Philomena and experienced an extraordinary cure. When this became known and publicised, devotion to the saint became widespread in France. Father Vianney, who had met Mme Jaricot when he was a curate with Fr Balley and would remain a loyal friend over the years, took up the devotion and encouraged it among his parishioners. Pauline Jaricot would suffer very greatly in her later years, as a former colleague made dishonest investments with the funds of the Society, losing large quantities of money that had been donated by devout – and mostly rather poor – people. Working to raise money to pay off the debts, and herself now reduced to penury, Mme Jaricot was a figure of humiliation and distress but Fr Vianney always recognised her as a saint. (Her cause for canonisation has been introduced and she is venerated as the foundress of the Society for the Propagation of the Faith, which today still supports missionaries worldwide.[6])

Miracles were frequently attributed to St Philomena, but the local people noted that it was their own Curé who first directed people to ask for her intercession. A little boy, paralysed from birth and unable to walk, was carried by his mother into the church as usual. "That child is too heavy for you" the Curé told her "Put him down and go and pray to St Philomena". She did, and the boy was cured.

At the heart of the Curé's message was a passionate insistence on people taking their faith seriously, praying daily, going to confession regularly, keeping Sunday holy. He was working at a time in history when the role and status of the Church in society was being seen in new ways. It was no longer, as it had been before the Revolution, part of the structures and fabric of the nation's system of government, with membership compulsory for anyone who held any sort of office. Nor was it now persecuted as it had been during the Terror and the days that followed. It was now claiming its place as fundamental to life itself – to God's original plan for the human race, and therefore for Ars.

In an important sense, Fr Vianney was at the forefront of a new era – a time when the Church could not assume that its structures be incorporated into those of the government and thus ensure that people heard God's message that way, but must be constantly part of people's daily lives with its own compelling and urgent message, calling to repentance, prayer, and the Sacraments.

There was now a new mood in Ars. Visitors noted its peaceful and happy atmosphere. There had been campaigns against the new Curé in the early days – spiteful gossip about him (sneering voices asserted that surely someone practising all those austerities and penances must have some dreadful sin to hide), attempts to get the Bishop to move him elsewhere. But now all that had stopped and if the ban on

Sunday work and on village dances seemed severe, the families seemed happy, neighbourly, friendly and welcoming.

"We must try to understand the complete and happy transformation which had taken place in Ars. Its people were one in piety, not only in outward observance but in refinement and behaviour. Their moral, mental and even physical development had deepened and strengthened. Peace of soul had brought serenity and calm... Many pilgrims bore witness to the quiet and peace that reigned in Ars. Its people were content and happy. When called upon, they rendered services graciously. This small town, lacking cabarets, was lived in by a smiling and joyful community which seemed to have achieved a golden age..."[7]

But this had been achieved not by the acceptance of a regime imposed by tradition and sealed into law and custom. Here a priest was working in post-revolutionary France and finding a new way: "...there had been no forcing. There was spoken and written testimony to prove this. A remarkable shaper of men had here created a type of villager who was sufficient unto himself, who carried with him his convictions and put them into practice wherever he went."[8]

Father Vianney recognised that his role as a priest was to bring people to God, to "snatch souls from their sin and to lead them back to love". As another great priest visiting Ars would put it over a hundred years later: "Men are free to adhere or not to faith and salvation; they claim this freedom and the Church for her part wishes them to take the step of faith in freedom from external constraints while safeguarding the moral obligation on each one to seek the truth and to hold onto it and act in accordance with his conscience ... But our love for mankind cannot be resigned to seeing them deprive themselves of salvation. We cannot directly produce the conversion of souls, but we are responsible for the proclamation of the Faith, of the totality of the Faith and of its demands. We must invite our faithful to conversion and to holiness; we must speak the truth, warn, advise, and make them desire the sacraments that re-establish them in the grace of God. The Curé d'Ars considered this a formidable but necessary ministry: 'If a pastor remains dumb when he sees God outraged and souls wandering away, woe to him!' We know with what care he prepared his Sunday homilies and his catechesis, and with what courage he recalled the requirements of the gospel, denounced sin and invited men to make good the evil they had committed."[9]

NOTES

1. Pope John Paul II on the Curé of Ars, Holy Thursday, 1986.
2. *The Curé d'Ars, portrait of a parish priest*, Lancelot Sheppard, London, Burns and Oates, 1958.

3. *The Curé of Ars and his Cross*, Jean de la Varende, 1958.
4. Ibid.
5. *The Curé d'Ars, portrait of a parish priest*, Lancelot Sheppard, London, Burns and Oates, 1953.
6. "By her faith, her trust, the force of her mind, her gentleness and her serene acceptance of all crosses, Pauline showed herself a true disciple of Christ." Pope John Paul II on Pauline Jaricot, in a letter to the Archbishop of Lyons, 1999, for celebrations in Lyons marking the bicentenary of her birth.
7. *The Curé of Ars and his Cross*, Jean de la Varende, 1958.
8. Ibid.
9. Pope John Paul II, Retreat for Priests at Ars, 1986.

CHAPTER FIVE

"Through John Mary Vianney, who consecrates his whole strength and his whole heart to him, Jesus saves souls. The Saviour entrusts them to him in abundance." [1]

~~~

The miracles, the hours spent in the confessional, the revival of faith, the school, the home for orphans and the teaching given there, the sermons, the commonsense counsel – word of what was happening in Ars began to spread. Not only were the local people coming to Mass and confession in full numbers, but people were beginning to come from further afield – much further afield – and soon the numbers would swell to extraordinary proportions.

The story of what happened at Ars now takes on its semi-legendary quality. The humble and holy parish priest of this obscure village became the heart of a massive revival that would affect the life of the Church in the whole of France in his lifetime and the worldwide Church in years to come.

It did not happen all at once. He began to be asked to help out with hearing confessions and preaching in nearby parishes, such as Montmerle and Chanceux. He invariably went on foot, and once there worked in his usual way, spending hours in the confessional, not resting, requiring no meals. At Trevoux in 1823 he preached a mission which had a profound effect, and at Limas a large number of his fellow clergy came to hear him and to join in praying before the Blessed Sacrament during the Forty Hours devotion.

People started to make the pilgrimage to Ars in order to go to confession to this remarkable priest of whom they had heard. On the face of things, there was nothing very remarkable when they got there. Father Vianney had certainly made the church look very beautiful and devotional, but it was nothing out of the ordinary architecturally. The village boasted no great array of pleasant coffee-shops in which to linger and chat. People went to Ars for just one main reason – to see the holy Curé and to be absolved of their sins. The Curé of Ars was known above all as a confessor.

Stories began to circulate – told by penitents themselves, who wanted to share something beautiful and remarkable that had happened to them. A criminal burdened by some horrible sins described how, when seriously ill, he finally decided to go to confession to the Curé – and made a rather specifically limited confession, deliberately omitting some of the worst things he had done. The Curé listened, asked if that were all, and on being told that it was, told him calmly and accurately, with dates and significant details, the sins that he had deliberately omitted. The man went away converted – and also found that his severe illness had vanished.

People were sometimes taken unawares. A

huntsman stood by the church with his gun and his dog, parading his lack of interest in what was happening within the building. The Curé, walking through on his way to the confessional, stopped and said, "A pity your soul is not as beautiful as your dog!", and the man, thunderstruck, recognised the voice of absolute truth. He went to confession, and learned that God had a completely new direction for his life – a year later, following his heart and grateful for the direction given by the Curé, he entered a Religious Order.

Others had similar experiences. A family group included a mother, grandmother, and daughter waited patiently in the crowd – a simple sign from the Curé indicated that the daughter should slip quietly forward ahead of the others in the confessional queue – unknown to everyone, she had something great on her conscience that she needed to unburden.

"Even before he was actually spoken to, the Curé knew what kind of soul he was dealing with. From the moment men came into his presence it was impossible to keep anything hidden. It was as though he had taken his stand in the very conscience of his penitents with clearer vision and better memory than themselves: almost he seemed to see and remember for them. If you tried to hide in the crowd, he came straight through the crowd. If with very little time to spare one were afraid of missing him, he seemed to hear the appeal which the penitent dared not utter aloud and would invite him to come ahead of his turn. It was exactly as though he held in his hand a thousand unseen threads linking him with everyone present, so that he had only to pull on the one he wanted, when he wanted. It was enough for him to raise his arm; the person he had in mind felt himself pointed at and obeyed the sign."[2]

How do we know these stories? People themselves simply told of their personal experiences. What had happened to them was not merely remarkable. It had brought them great relief and joy – even at the cost of initial humiliation – and they wanted others to receive what they had received. Forgiveness and absolution are not joyless things. To discover the greatness of God's love and mercy is a wonderful experience, and the fact that people felt able to talk about it, even if it meant revealing information about themselves that would otherwise be humiliating, is significant. The way to Heaven is a road that passes through penance and sorrow for sin – and it is a road for which human beings are made, giving a direction for life, which is in the end a happy thing, something of great goodness which people do want to share.

Many years later a Pope would speak of "the gaunt figure of John Baptist Vianney, with that head shining with long hair that resembled a snowy crown, and that thin face, wasted from long fasting, where the innocence and holiness of the meekest and humblest of souls shone forth so clearly that the first sight of it called crowds of people back to thoughts of salvation."[3]

Not everyone was comfortable with the Curé's approach. Sinners who were genuine and repentant found relief and joy in absolution and a new relationship with God. But those who went to the famous Curé certain of their own special spiritual needs and concerns and relishing the prospect of a long personal discussion centred on a sense of their being a chosen soul, found themselves treated with a brisk approach which they did not enjoy. "Talk to your own confessor about this – he knows your needs better than I" was the advice given to one such lady, and others were told: "Well, say such-and-such a prayer, and forget about all of that". They didn't like it. Letters arrived denouncing him as ignorant and lacking in theological knowledge and gossip spread about how unhelpful he was, how poor in judgement of deeply spiritual people.

There was of course also jealousy among some of the other clergy and this, coupled with dissatisfaction from those who felt they had received inadequate attention from him, culminated in the drawing up a petition for his removal from the parish. A copy was sent to him – perhaps by a well-wisher wanting him to know what was going on, or perhaps by some one with the opposite intention of causing him distress. His response was immediate – he signed it and posted it on to the organisers. He was perfectly genuine and sincere in thanking, too, those of his priest colleagues who reproached him or found fault with what he was doing: he believed that he was inadequate, a sinner unworthy of the huge grace of priesthood and not doing as much as he should to save his own soul and those of his parishioners and penitents.

He was not moved from the parish and the crowds continued to come, in larger and larger numbers. France was changing. The railway had arrived – and this meant that what was once an obscure village was now within reach of all the country's main towns and cities. The railway company started to offer special return tickets which were valid for a week – because the crowds meant that people might have to wait that long to get to confession to the Curé. Coaches met the special trains, and took people to Ars, where hotels were now being opened, and where the local people also offered accommodation in their houses.

At the heart of this was a man who ate little, barely slept, and imposed severe penances on himself so that everyday comforts played no part in his life at all. Father Vianney rose at one in the morning, after less than two hours sleep, and went into the already crowded church with a lantern. People were waiting, as they had been waiting all the previous day and night. He began by praying in the chancel, and then went to the confessional, where he heard confessions throughout the early hours of the morning, until he celebrated Mass at 6am. Then, with the day's main work still ahead of him, he would be thronged with people who wanted his advice, or asked him to bless their rosaries, or their children, or someone who was sick. At eight o'clock he went to La Providence, where he drank a small glass of milk, and then he went back to the task of hearing confessions. This was broken only by the saying of his Office at 10am and then another visit to La Providence for the morning catechism class – his great joy – at 11am, and this would be followed by the Angelus. He would then try to walk to his house, but this was not easy through the thick crowds – people by now were packing out the town square in the hopes of getting near to him. His midday meal consisted of cold boiled potatoes. The kindly ladies who at various times tried to cook for him and give him adequate nourishment invariably failed in their objective. He politely declined the food, or sometimes would not even open the door to allow them to bring it in. He boiled up some potatoes at the beginning of each week, and ate just a couple each day, and that was that.

Father Vianney was now rarely alone. Even as he seized fifteen minutes at midday to eat cold potatoes, he was besieged by people who wanted to talk to him, to confide their worries, to ask advice. As he walked back to the church, as he left the pulpit after preaching, as he headed for the confessional, people wanted to touch him, or tried to snip tiny pieces off his cassock or vestments as souvenirs. Even getting his hair cut presented problems – he had to bring the cuttings home and burn then, or otherwise they would have been taken as souvenirs.

He would not have his photograph taken, or his likeness painted or drawn – not that this made any difference to souvenir sellers in the town, who were by now selling small cards depicting him – and he would not allow himself to be given any honour or treated in any way as a celebrity. His shabby cassock and much-mended boots were sometimes discussed by other clergy, who felt that he was not giving the clerical state the social status that was its due, although it had to be admitted that he was always clean and neat.

His humility was genuine and had nothing unpleasant or cloying about it. He spoke without affectation about himself as a poor sinner and as a priest who was not doing enough for God, whose love and kindness and mercy were so great. He spoke often and in the most down-to-earth way, about Heaven and Hell. Death comes to us all: our ultimate destiny matters. Could anything be more terrible than an eternity of suffering in Hell? Of course not. A priest must fix his sights on heaven, and get as many there as possible during the span of life allotted to him. To do less than this was to risk one's own eternal salvation.

In the pulpit, John Vianney's voice was not loud or spectacular and he did not have a witty or splendid way of speaking. On the contrary, his voice was light and quite high-pitched. He spoke in ordinary simple words that everyone could understand. His great emphasis was on the greatness of God's love and the horror of unrepented sin. Christ's presence in the Tabernacle was the great reality to which he drew people's attention continually, gesturing from the pulpit and speaking of Christ with great tenderness.

His sermons were above all about personal sin and its avoidance. He did not allow anyone to have the comfortable feeling that it was enough to go through some sort of outward form of Christianity, sitting through a sermon or attending Mass out of habit and because of social convention, without allowing the message to penetrate the soul. "Unfortunately, such a large body of Christians do not know themselves and do not even try to know themselves. They follow routines and habits, and they do not want to see reason. They are blind, and they move along in their blindness. If a priest wants to tell them about the state they are in, they do not listen, and if they go through the pretence of listening, they will do nothing about what they are told. This state, my dear people, is the most unhappy state that anyone can possibly imagine, and perhaps the most dangerous one as well…"[4]

He did not allow people to feel a sense of superiority on account of their Faith. In an era where perhaps some felt a comfortably smug antagonism towards Jews, as being outside the Church, he issued a direct challenge: "We can see that the Jews had formed an idea of their Redeemer which did not conform with the state of austerity in which he appeared. It seemed as if they could not persuade themselves that this could indeed be he who was to be their Saviour. Saint Paul tells us very clearly that if the Jews had recognised him as God, they would never have put him to death... But what excuse can we make, my dear brethren, for the coldness and the contempt which we show towards Jesus Christ? Oh yes, we do truly believe that Jesus Christ came on earth, that he provided the most convincing proofs of his divinity. Hence the reason for our hope... But, tell me, with all this, what homage do we really pay him? Do we do more for him than if we did not believe all this? Tell me, dear brethren, does our conduct corresponded at all to our beliefs? We are wretched creatures."[5]

He was very emphatic about the evil of back-biting and gossip and would give examples of the way people speak when they are doing this, using expressions like "Oh, everyone says so!" and "Oh, it's well known!" while spreading gossip about some one's drinking, or work habits, or finances. Giving an example of how people like to draw an evil inference even when someone is doing good, he told the story of St Nicholas – which would have been familiar to his listeners as he was then, as now, a popular saint associated with gifts at Christmas-time – walking at night around the house of three young girls who did not have a good reputation. "And yet, this bishop, who would certainly have been condemned by you, was indeed a very great saint and most dear to God.

What he was doing was the best deed in the world. In order to spare these young people the shame of begging, he went in the night and threw money in to them through their window because he feared it was poverty which had made them abandon themselves to sin."

Degradation of young people, and the spreading among them of habits of bad language or sexually explicit jokes and talk, was something that drew strong rebukes from Fr Vianney in the pulpit. "There is nothing more abominable, nothing more horrible, than such talk... Can the Christian really afford to occupy his mind with such horrible images, a Christian who is a temple of the Holy Spirit, a Christian who has been sanctified by the Body and precious Blood of Jesus Christ?" He emphasised that parents must take full responsibility for their children, in teaching them what is right and in protecting them from bad company.

Father Vianney knew about everyday life on the farms and in the village. People had to work hard and it was tempting to get slack about, for example, ensuring proper modesty in dressing and undressing before others, or about adequate privacy and separate sleeping arrangements for young men and young women. "But, you will say to me, if we had to do all the things you say, there would be an awful lot of work to do. My friends, it is work that you must do, and if you do not do it, you will be punished on account of it..."[6]

The little orphanage, "La Providence", flourished, and to the Curé it became perhaps the place he loved best. He had raised the funds for the building and worked with his own hands to get it completed. It was here that his prayers brought some of the miracles that would be described again and again as word of them spread. In addition to the multiplication of grain in the incident already mentioned, there was another occasion a few years later when the cook found that she simply did not have enough flour to bake the bread she needed for supper. There was just a tiny amount left, barely a spoonful when she put it in the bowl. He told her to pray, add water, and keep on kneading. Then set it aside to let it rise as usual. She did so, and when she returned there was a massive quantity of dough, more than enough for all their needs – as she kneaded it, it spilled out from the wooden container and out on to the floor. On another day, Fr Vianney himself was helping to serve the children's lunch. The children were hungry, and although there was not very much in the bowl, he ladled out generously. As the last child was fed, there was still a good deal left.

La Providence was a home to many little girls over the years. But, concerned for its long-term future, the Bishop decided that its care should be given over to the Sisters of St Joseph, who, in 1847, decided that it should be simply a school, rather than an orphanage. This distressed Fr Vianney, but he accepted the decision, even though it meant a personal loss to him – he had been able to go there as a place of refuge and welcome. The three women who had originally helped to run it, Jeanne-Marie Chanay, Catherine Lassagne, and Marie Filliat, continued to work for Fr Vianney in the parish. "M. Vianney bore no grudge against the new sisters. They were not dependent on him, but he visited them; inaugurated their chapel; received the renewal of their vows. The parish school for girls prospered, like the boys' school, directed by Brother Athanasius. He rejoiced at it – but it was no longer his house. It had been the one attachment remaining in his heart to a thing here on earth; and God broke it suddenly, ruthlessly, leaving his servant only the pulpit, the confessional and the altar."[7]

But the children who had been taught by Fr Vianney never forgot what they had learned. When preaching to children, he kept things simple, and of course this appealed to adults too. In avoiding sin in daily life, he advised them, "Do only what you can offer to God". A simple and straightforward approach to the day's work and joys.

Brother Athanasius, mentioned above, arrived in Ars at Fr Vianney's invitation in 1849 with a team of other Brothers to start a school for boys. He became a great support to the Curé, acting as a secretary and running the parish choir. When numbers of visitors began to swell, he was in charge of organising them and making some semblance of order among the great crowds.

A difficulty endured by Fr Vianney was that of his assistant, Fr Raymond. He arrived full of fresh ideas and a great sense of energy, took over the main room – from then on, Fr Vianney was to sleep in a small dark room downstairs – and initially appeared to believe that he was to take over the parish completely. He was a gifted and intelligent man with a fine voice and a noted preaching style. Only when the local people objected did he finally restore Fr Vianney to his due place – including his proper room – and go to lodge in the village. But his officious style and his interference in all parish matters continued and he made life difficult for his parish priest at every turn. Father Vianney, however, would hear no complaints against him, spoke up for him when there was any criticism and wrote him a note of warm thanks when, after eight years, he was finally sent elsewhere. When his replacement proved to be more helpful, open, hard-working and pleasant, Fr Vianney seemed to miss Fr Raymond's nagging and said that the new man did not rebuke him enough. He had seen in Fr Raymond a useful cross which he could carry as Christ carried his.

NOTES

1. Pope John Paul II, Holy Thursday, 1986
2. *The Secret of the Curé d'Ars*, Henry Gheon. Translated by F.J. Sheed. London, Sheed and Ward, 1946.

3. Pope Pius XI, on canonising St John Vianney, 1925.
4. *Sermons of the Curé of Ars*, tr, Una Morrissey, 1960 Henry Regnery Co. Current edition TAN Books USA.
5. Ibid.
6. Ibid.
7. *The Secret of the Curé d'Ars*, Henri Gheon, Sheed and Ward 1946.

CHAPTER SIX

Virtue demands courage, constant effort and, above all, help from on high.[1]

~ ~ ~

One of the oddest aspects of the extraordinary story of St John Vianney is the part played by the powers of evil.

Father John Vianney was a man doing good. He was bringing people to God, reconciling people who had been away from the Church, giving absolution to the repentant, teaching children the truths of the Catholic Faith. The conversion of a village had proved a catalyst for the conversion of first hundreds, and then thousands, of other people. He did this with prayer, fasting, and personal penances.

It is a fundamental part of the Christian faith that Satan exists. Quoting the Scriptures (Gen 3:1-5, Wis 2:24) the Catechism of the Catholic Church speaks of a "seductive voice, opposed to God", who is a "fallen angel" called "Satan" or "the Devil" (Jn 8:44, Rev 12:9). The Catechism goes on "Scripture witnesses to the disastrous influence of the one Jesus calls 'a murderer from the beginning', who would even try to divert Jesus from the mission received from his Father" (Jn 8:44 cf. Mt 4:1-11).[2] The Catechism quotes St John Damascene: "The reason the Son of God appeared was to destroy the works of the Devil."

Such a being would naturally want to thwart the work being done by a good and holy priest. During his time at Ars, John Vianney began to experience just such attacks. They were specific, vicious and physical. There were unexplained noises at night, shrieking and cursing, the sound of feet on the stairs when there was no one there, even outbreaks of fire. Voices called out, mocking the priest: "Vianney! Potato-eater! We've got you!" A picture of the Annunciation was covered in filth.

At first, Fr Vianney would later recall, he thought the disturbance was caused by a rat and he shook the curtains and rummaged about with a pitchfork to find the animal. One night there was a great rattling at the door and windows and he called out "Who is there?" but found no one – and although there was thick snow, no footprints were to be seen. Thinking that thieves might be intent on stealing some of the new items for the church which the family from the manor had recently provided, he asked two men from the village to stay in the presbytery for a couple of nights to help ward off any intruders. They became convinced that the noises and disruptions were not of human origin.

Father Vianney even gave a nickname to his adversary "the grappin". "He never minded speaking of the devil. In the first place, he thought that to speak of him contemptuously would be one sure blow to his pride, for tricks of this sort seemed to the Curé too absurd to bring any glory, even to the victim, much less to their inventor. Again, he bore witness before men – who have fallen into a perilous scepticism on the point – of the harsh reality of the world of evil spirits…"[3]

John Vianney prayed, making the Sign of the Cross. He noted, he later reported, that Satan seemed most active when something good was going to happen: "the louder grew the din, the happier was the Curé, for he had noticed that this was the signal that a great sinner was coming to him, under the impulse of God's grace; invariably he found on the next day that his net held 'a big fish'."[4]

So the work continued. Father Vianney remained convinced of his own complete unworthiness and ineptitude as a parish priest. Twice, he tried to leave the parish – once to return to the family home, and once to join a Trappist monastery. On the first occasion he was brought back, and on the second prevented from leaving, by people from the village. They loved him now, and they wanted to keep him. He was, as he had told the young boy he would do on his first arrival, "showing them the way to Heaven".

He looked frail and ill, though always cheerful and smiling, and one day in May 1843 he fainted during morning prayers in the church. He had pneumonia – hardly surprising in view of his scant sleep, minimal food, and harsh penances. He submitted to medical attention and care, and was taken to bed.

The Bishop sent a replacement to take over parish duties and meanwhile the people prayed, lighting candles, weeping, and sending up to Fr Vianney's room quantities of medals, rosaries and holy pictures for him to bless. These had to be brought in great baskets, and he willingly blessed them, although he was unable to rise from his bed and had to do so lying down.

It seemed almost certain that he was dying, and the priest from the nearby parish of Jassans came to anoint him and bring the Viaticum, the "food for the journey", the last Communion to be received before death. The doctor pronounced sadly that Fr Vianney would last "another thirty minutes, no more". But, as Fr Vianney was later to explain, he felt he could not appear before God "empty-handed". He had done so little. He must bring more souls to salvation. He prayed fervently. He had promised St Philomena "a hundred Masses" of thanksgiving if his life was spared. He had asked that people in the church light a great candle before her statue.

He recovered. Those gathered round the bed the next morning saw that he seemed to smile at someone, and he whispered, very quietly, the name "Philomena" several times. Then, a few moments later, he said to M. Pertinand, the village schoolmaster, who was nearest to him "My friend – I am cured!" And he was.

It was after this that he sought to return to his family home for a few days, only to be brought back by a large delegation from the village who effectively besieged the house, saying that they could not go to confession except to him, that they loved him and needed him. It was clear that wherever he went, Ars would follow him. Ars would be wherever he was. He returned, and as he did so the parish bells rang and the entire village came out to welcome him, people leaving their work and all normal activity stopping, as he returned to his house, giving blessings all along the way.

Honours were coming his way, and he disliked that very much. In 1850, when he was made a Canon, he wore the formal silk and ermine cape only once, at the initiating ceremony when it was placed upon him, and then never again. In due course he sold it and gave the money to charity. Later the Emperor, Napoleon III, wanted to make him a member of the Legion of Honour. Local people were thrilled. The citation read "The confidence of the population in Monsieur the Curé of Ars is boundless: it is that angelic faith that moves mountains. Several occurrences are cited which it would be hard to explain on natural grounds." But Fr Vianney was not interested. When told of the honour, he asked if it would mean money for the poor. No, he was told – it was just an honour for him personally. In that case, he said, please, no. But to no avail: it came anyway, although he would not let anyone pin the actual cross to his cassock. He did all this in such a matter-of-fact way that people enjoyed laughing over the incident.

The work went on, and by now people were writing down and passing on the commonsense advice he gave them, the encouragement, the wisdom, the good cheer and the reminders to penitence.

"When you go to confession, you must understand what you are about to do; you are about to un-nail Our Lord."

"Everything is a reminder of the Cross. We ourselves are made in the shape of a cross."

"We should make the sign of the cross with great reverence. We begin with the head – that is the chief, the creation, the Father; then the heart, love, life, redemption, the Son; then the shoulders, strength, the Holy Spirit."

"Nothing is so contrary to charity as pride."

"Since we are only in the world for God himself, we shall never be happy if we do not serve him with zeal and love."

"We must honour God as he requires us to honour him, or we shall be asked why."

"The saints did not all begin well, but they all ended well."

"Those who love riches or pleasures offer God nothing but the languid remains of a heart worn out in the service of the world."

His way of teaching about prayer was simple. He suggested things that everyone could do: "When you wake in the night, transport yourself quickly in the spirit before the Tabernacle, and say: Behold me, my God, I come to adore you, to praise, thank, and love you, and to keep you company with all the angels."

"When we pray, we should open our hearts to God, like a fish when it sees the wave coming."

He gave common sense advice about sin and temptation: "We must watch over our mind, our heart and our senses, for these are the gates by which the devil enters in."

"Offer your temptations for the conversion of sinners. When the devil sees you doing this, he is beside himself with rage and makes off, because then the temptation is turned against himself."

He was able to talk to people who wanted to seek God, or to return to church after a long absence, or who did not know how to pray: "If you set out to meet God, he will come to meet you."

By now, the huge crowds had become part of the routine of work. In the year 1858, some 80,000 people flocked to the village. Ars was recognised as a centre of spiritual renewal and pilgrimages were part of the life of the region. Every sort of person came, the rich and well-to-do jostling with poorer people who trudged on foot. The sick and the handicapped were brought for blessings. There were stories of dramatic cures, although the Curé always hurried away and did not want to talk about such things. In his sermons, he emphasised the value of suffering: it was not pointless, but a form of unity with Christ. Offered to Christ and with Christ, it was redemptive, could win souls for Heaven.

"Here is an exact account of the numbers of

pilgrims coming to Ars, and their behaviour. The first records are from Monsieur des Garets, the nephew of the one we already know, who had inherited the property and manor house of his aunt and who had been elected Mayor of Ars. 'The numbers of pilgrims increased yearly from 1830 to 1845 when they reached their maximum, three to four hundred a day. In the Parrèche depot, the most important of Lyons, a special office was kept open to sell tickets for Ars, with the notice added that the ticket was good for eight days.' And M. des Garets adds, showing what the crowds were like, 'It was well known that a certain amount of time was needed to reach the Curé in order to have a word with him or get absolution.' Francois Pertinard was the hotel-keeper and owner of a daily coach service between Ars and Lyons, and a three times a week service between Trevous and Ars. Two coaches also ran between Villefranche and Ars, and a fifth coach left and returned daily to Villefranche. The drivers estimated at eighty-thousand the number of pilgrims who had come by that means in the last year of the saint's life, which indicates that the means of travel had been many times increased by that time bringing the number up to a hundred, or a hundred and twenty thousand persons."[5]

John Vianney now looked very elderly and frail. People noticed his large eyes, deep-set and sparkling, in his thin face. His hair was very sparse. His penances and his severe illnesses had given him the look of a person who seemed at times almost transparent.

In 1854 Archbishop William Ullathorne visited Ars. Ullathorne was himself a remarkable man, who worked for some years in Australia as a chaplain among the convicts and was instrumental, through the report he subsequently wrote, in helping to get the cruel policy of transportation ended and Australia established as a colony on a more humane basis. His visit to Ars came after he had returned to Britain and was appointed Archbishop of Birmingham following the restoration of Catholic hierarchy in 1850. Ullathorne described vividly the simplicity of Ars and the Curé's house: "The walls were naked and ruinous; there was scarcely anything there besides the poor furniture in his own room and his little bed… Before he came in I was told he would escape from me as soon as he could for a little solitude. But no. His manner of receiving me was as free and simple as it was full of humility and charity. There was nothing of a tone and gesture straining itself to maintain a character, but the disengaged self-abandonment and simple politeness of a saint." Ullathorne asked for Vianney's prayers for Catholics in England and the Curé told him "I believe the Church in England will return to its ancient splendour…", echoing the view of many in Europe. Ullathorne also went to confession to the Curé and found him a wise and kindly confessor: "At each point which tended to a question his words were few, simple, penetrating, but exceedingly large in their charity… With him the Spirit is everything, the form and manner of action of little consideration, so long as God is the object of the soul… On one practical point he gave a practical decision. It was precise, clear, and satisfying. He knelt by my side when he had concluded, as he did before he began, and I felt it was a moment of grace."[6]

There is a touching description of a visit, in early 1859, of Pauline Jaricot, by now impoverished and ill, weighed down with a burden of debt and regarded by many as a failure and even an embarrassment to the Church. "In the cold February of 1859 she arrived in Ars with a companion; both women were cold, wet through and hungry. The east wind was blowing and snow was on the ground. Abbé Vianney welcomed them in his room where with some damp logs he endeavoured to make a fire, but no sooner was it lit than it went out again. 'Don't worry about the cold' Pauline besought him 'but please warm my poor soul with a few sparks of faith and hope.'"[7]

The image of these two devout and dedicated people, warmed only by their faith, in a damp cold room on a February day, is a vivid one. Neither would know material comforts again. Pauline would later record how the kindness of her old friend did indeed warm her heart.

John Vianney had always been content to be poor. "He warned that the needy were never to be spurned, since a disregard for them would reach in turn to God. When beggars knocked at his door, he received them with love and was very happy to be able to say to them 'I am living in need myself; I am one of you.' And towards the end of his life, he used to enjoy saying things like this: 'I will be happy when I go; for now I no longer have any possessions and so when God in his goodness sees fit to call me, I will be ready and willing to go.'"[8]

Later that year, death came for the Curé of Ars. In the stifling heat of French summers, he had remained in the small church, hour after hour sitting in a small confessional, in a cramped building where the crowds made the air heavy and humid. In the summer of 1859 the heat was intense. At one point the 73-year-old Curé had to be taken out for some air. He was persuaded to have some sips of wine. Earlier, he had fallen on the stairs while making his way to the church in the dark.

The local people had known for some weeks that he was getting very frail. On the feast of Corpus Christi he was unable to carry the monstrance in procession, and simply raised it in a blessing. He could not preach much now. He would stand in the pulpit, but communicate mainly by gesture – pointing towards the tabernacle with great love and tenderness. But he still heard confessions for some sixteen or seventeen hours a day, beginning in the darkness of the very early hours, after scarcely any sleep.

When he was finally persuaded to return to his bed for what were to be his last hours, crowds gathered beneath the window. They wanted to know when he was blessing them, so it was arranged that when he raised his frail hand to do so, a bell would be rung. The Sisters of St Joseph tended to him, and because he was too frail to resist they slipped a mattress beneath him so that he was no longer lying on a hard plank.

John Vianney had always had no fear of death, except that it meant facing God and having to account for the years he had spent as a priest and for the souls entrusted to his care. He had preached "Our home is Heaven. On earth we are like travellers staying at an hotel. When one is away, one is always thinking of going home."[9]

He lay for four days, praying. He was anointed and given the Viaticum. The Bishop came. At two in the morning the Curé gently died, while a fellow-priest was reciting the Church's Prayers for the Dying from the prayer-book, and a great thunderstorm was raging outside.

NOTES

1. Patience of the Curé of Ars. *Thoughts of the Curé d'Ars*, TAN Books, USA.
2. Catechism of the Catholic Church, 394.
3. *The Secret of the Curé of Ars*, Henri Gheon. Sheed and Ward 1934.
4. Ibid.
5. *The Curé of Ars and his Cross*, Jean de la Varende, 1958.

6. From Letters of Archbishop Ullathorne, London 1892, quoted in *The Curé of Ars, portrait of a parish priest*, Lancelot Sheppard, London Burns and Oates 1958.
7. *The Curé of Ars, portrait of a parish priest*, Lancelot Sheppard London Burns and Oates 1958.
8. Pope John XXIII, *Sacerdoti Primordia*, 1959. The quotes from St John Vianney in this are from the Processus in the Vatican Archives, v. 227.
9. On Detachment. *Thoughts of the Curé d'Ars,* TAN Books USA.

CHAPTER SEVEN

From this noble place that contrasts with the previous simplicity of the original village, I give thanks to Jesus Christ for this unheard-of gift of the priesthood, that of the Curé of Ars and that of all the priests of yesterday and today. They prolong the sacred ministry of Jesus Christ throughout the world. In the Christian communities they are like the frontier posts of the mission, they work often in difficult, hidden, thankless conditions, for the salvation of souls and for the spiritual renewal of the world, which sometimes honours them and sometimes ignores them, disregards them, or persecutes them. Today, in union with all the bishops of the world... I pay them the homage that they deserve, praying God to sustain them and reward them.[1]

~~~

A parish priest had died. Thousands of people wanted to record how he had helped them: advice in discerning a life's vocation, a promise of a problem resolved, the healing of some disease or painful condition. There were stories galore of concealed sins revealed in confession, kindly advice given briskly and with a gentle smile, a stern message delivered just when it was needed.

"A procession of three hundred priests and religious, and six thousand pilgrims escorted the coffin to the church for the Requiem on Sunday. Directly behind the body walked Antoine Givre. An eternity and a day before, when he guided the Curé and his cart to the village, he had been the first of the people to hear the voice 'My young friend, you have shown me the way to Ars; I will show you the way to Heaven.' On 14 August 1859, the remains of the Curé d'Ars were lowered into a vault in the middle of the church."[2]

John Vianney was beatified in 1905 and canonised by Pope Pius XI, in May 1925. The process for this had been opened in 1866, waiving the normal rule which decreed that a certain number of years after death must pass before anything could be done.

John Vianney has been a consistently popular saint for a hundred and fifty years – more, if you include the love and veneration that was shown to him during his lifetime. Perhaps it is because people like stories of miracles and healings and a saint overcoming the horrible activities of Satan. And we all rather relish hearing about people's sinfulness being revealed by a holy confessor, about godless people being reproached and having to convert, about a bleak community undergoing a massive spiritual renewal. But the message of his life is rather more uncomfortable than that: he understood the role of a priest to be that of bringing souls to God, and that means your soul and mine, not just the souls of people in books and pamphlets, in stories cosily distanced from our own lives.

In 1929, St John Vianney was formally declared the patron saint of parish priests across the world, by Pope Pius XI, who celebrated his own 50th anniversary as a priest that year. In 2009, on the 150th anniversary of the saint's death, Pope Benedict XVI, in announcing a "Year for Priests" dedicated the year to him.

What was the legacy that St John Vianney left to the Church in France, and to the world? As a model of priestly zeal he is in a sense timeless. It is true that many of the details with which he was involved – local dances, people stealing from one another's fields, money spent in taverns that should have gone to the family budget – seem dated now. But in essentials things don't change: we still need to be alerted to the wrongfulness of some forms of entertainment, stealing is still wrong even if it is from a supermarket rather than an orchard, and if drunkards no longer impoverish their families they still make life miserable for them. Styles of preaching change; it is not fashionable to speak of Hell at present, but that doesn't mean it isn't there and doesn't deserve a mention.

In some aspects, St John Vianney is surprisingly modern. The need to confess sin is ever-present, and the TV "reality show" or the "counsellor" offering some form of talk-it-through therapy has none of the absolute secrecy of the confessor and of course cannot give absolution. Nor has it yet been proved that encouraging people to shed all notion of guilt actually makes for human happiness. Many people would find the idea of a wise, holy – and perhaps comfortingly elderly! – confessor, steeped in prayer and living a life of personal austerity, very beautiful, helpful, and consoling. Certainly, one of the common features of all the New Movements in the Church (Focolare, the charismatics and their various linked groups, the Neo-Catechumenate, and, in Britain, the Faith Movement and Youth 2000) is a revival of commitment to confession. A feature of some of the gatherings of such groups is the personal testimony given by people who have returned to this Sacrament after a long absence, or who have been introduced to it in adulthood after inadequate catechesis at a Catholic school.

Saint John Vianney stood aside from all political and national debate and action in his lifetime. He studiously avoided getting involved in any attempt to seek debate about pre-Revolutionary ideas of Church and State, and simply concentrated on what God had called him to do – being a parish priest. He was passionately committed to the service of the poor, frequently preached on the need to be generous, gave away all funds that came his way and denounced greed and the building up of riches – but he did not suggest that Christ had come to establish an earthly kingdom centred on a political creed. On the contrary, he pointed always to Heaven – and one of his pleas to the rich was that they would have difficulty in getting there if they did not abandon idleness and luxury and do all they could to serve their fellow-men, especially the poorest.

There is no getting away from it: St John Vianney simply challenges us all. In today's Church, he is a reminder of the value of the priest in a parish, doing work which seems obscure but which is actually central in getting people to Heaven. He was loyal to the Church, to his Bishop, and to Rome. He treated people with courtesy, men and women alike, and did not create cliques or favour factions within the parish. It is notable that he had a good working relationship with women, and respected their enthusiasm and their talents: in fact his closest collaborators in Ars were women – the three with whom he initiated the orphanage and school at "La Providence", the lady at the manor who supported his work. To men and women alike he was blunt in his call to live by God's moral law, frank about the demands made by the Christian life and insistent about the need for prayer, regular confession, and respect for Sunday as belonging to God.

While very much alert to the everyday lives of the people he sought to serve, he was not really a man of his age: he took no apparent interest in the great issues of the day, not even in things that actually affected his village, such as the coming of the railway. He did not pronounce on political issues, even local ones, although his preaching meant that people's lives were radically changed and this had social consequences. His message was always focused on eternity – on living life well here in order to spend the rest of it with God. Towards the end of his life he was often asked about prophecies that were being widely discussed, especially concerning various claimants to the throne of France, rumours of a restoration of the monarchy, coupled with predictions of dire calamities (famines, pestilence), and sundry conspiracy theories. He always refused to have anything to do with any of these. In 1855 Canon R. Smith, of Penrith, visited Ars on behalf of the president of the seminary at Ushaw. Canon Smith was able to obtain the advice requested about the seminary's future and also took the opportunity to enquire about certain other matters, reporting back about the Curé: "It is certain that he has not ever foretold any bad times coming, and never speaks of the present times – refusing to have anything whatever to do with politics, at least as far as giving opinions to the public."[3]

The teaching of the Curé of Ars – although connected with the drama of his life with its austerities, its dramatic miracles and battles with evil – has a message which is essentially one of balance, of being rooted in what is true and wise and lasting. He was not taken in by factions, and he always saw the real drama of life as a battle between good and evil, with Christ always calling people to the good and the true, and a priest being at the heart of this mission. We cannot imagine him announcing himself as a Lefebvrist or leaning towards sedevacantism, or joining groups to murmur dissent from Humanae Vitae, or speculating about why there should be priestesses. His mission was one of saving souls – souls here and now, in the place to which he had been assigned.

John Vianney died before the First Vatican Council began its work – a Council that had been called to tackle the theological, moral and spiritual issues raised by the turbulent events of the nineteenth century. It affirmed the Church's teachings, defined Papal Infallibility for all time and ensured that an understanding of the Church as a rock of stability was given to the faithful. But its work was interrupted by the Franco-Prussian War – which in turn was followed by the First and Second World Wars, so it was almost a century later that a Second Vatican Council was called, which had to tackle the question of how to present the great truths of the Faith following far more turbulent times than any nineteenth-century cleric could have envisaged.

But this holy parish priest is still able to speak to Catholics today, across all those years marked by war, and massive social change. His popularity has not waned. Today pilgrims still go to Ars, and people come from places he could never have imagined would know about the small village – from Australia and America, from eastern Europe and from Asia.

In Ars today there is a Basilica and all the trimmings of an established place of pilgrimage. But "the presbytery has preserved something of the essential Abbé Vianney, the peasant-style house, the rough walls, the poor possessions, the few books, the large breviary. The shrine in the church contains the body, though it is vested in a cassock of silk, a rochet of lace such as he never would have worn and his hands are clasping a bejewelled rosary such as he would have given away on the spot. But the face is preserved by its mask of wax and you can look on those features as they were at the end of his life – the long straight line of the mouth, the face of a man tried and proved by suffering, the eyes just perceptible through the thin lids, the long, finely wrought nose, but the face of a man who found peace through following his vocation, though sorely tempted to abandon it for the peace of monastic life… The man appears almost to glow through the wax covering of the features. It seems to be the light of holiness shining through the dead shell."[4]

In choosing St John Vianney as the patron of a year dedicated to priests, Pope Benedict is challenging us all to be holy, hard-working, self-sacrificing, open to conversion and repentance and to a renewed understanding of the sacraments. It is rather agreeable to read – and to write – about a deeply holy priest who lived quite a long time ago, who grew up in a France torn by revolution, who came to a parish and transformed it, who was loved and lovable, who preached great and challenging truths and was so close to God that he became almost physically translucent with God's light. But the story is actually a down-to-earth one for us all. He was a parish priest and he did what parish priests are meant to do. We are all made for Heaven and we won't get there if we sin and neglect our prayers. The story of St John Vianney is not essentially a charming tale of a rural priest of a long time ago. It's an uncomfortable reminder of the things that really matter.

In 1959 Pope John XXIII issued an encyclical letter about St John Vianney, mentioning in particular his chastity, his prayer life, his obedience to his bishop, and his complete commitment to the priesthood in the service of his parish. "He proved to be a tireless worker for God, one who was wise and devoted in winning over young people and bringing families back to the standards of Christian morality, a worker who was never too tired to show an interest in the human needs of his flock, one whose own way of life was very close to theirs and who was prepared to exert every effort and make any sacrifice to establish Christian schools and make missions available to the people; and all of these things show that St John Vianney reproduced the true image of the good shepherd in himself as he dealt with the flock entrusted to his care for he knew his sheep, protected them from dangers and gently but firmly looked after them."

Pope John also emphasised John Vianney's voluntary poverty and concern for the poor, his willingness to share or give away what he had. "He was rich in his generosity towards others but the poorest of men in dealing with himself; he passed a life that was almost completely detached from the changeable, perishable goods of this world, and his spirit was free and unencumbered by impediments of this kind, so that it could always lie open to those who suffered from any kind of misery; and they flocked from everywhere to seek his consolation."[5] Pope John emphasised the importance of John Vianney as an example and model for priests, a theme echoed by all the Popes who have spoken about him.

"The Curé of Ars is a model of priestly zeal for all pastors" Pope John Paul II wrote in 1986, on the second centenary of the saint's birth. "The secret of his generosity is to be found without doubt in his love for God, lived without limits, in constant response to the love manifest in Christ crucified. This is where he bases his desire to do everything to save the souls ransomed by Christ at such a great price and to bring them back to the love of God."[6] Pope John Paul recalled St John Vianney's "pithy sayings" and quoted many of them, and also noted his courage in denouncing evil and the gentleness with which he showed the powerful and attractive side of virtue. In giving systematic Christian instruction in regular classes, he appealed to both children and adults, giving both a "matchless testimony which flowed from his heart." And all of this was centred on a great devotion to the Eucharist, a great love of the Mass and a profound sense of the reality of Christ's presence in the Tabernacle. "It was generally before the tabernacle that he spent long hours in adoration, before daybreak or in the evening; it was towards the tabernacle that he often turned in his homilies, saying with emotion: 'He is there!'"[7]

In October 1986, Pope John Paul visited Ars. Some of the French clergy had signed a letter begging him not to do this, as they considered that the saint venerated there was no longer a useful model for the priesthood. But the Pope from Poland, whose own priesthood had matured in the difficult days of Communist rule and whose Petrine ministry embraced a new generation growing up in a world facing so many uncertainties, had a great devotion to this holy and humble parish priest. He led a retreat for priests at Ars, focusing directly and in detail on the specifics that set a priest apart from other men.

"Our priesthood is rooted in the missions of the Divine Person, in their mutual gift in the heart of the Holy Trinity… Our mission is a mission of salvation… Following the apostles, we are associated in a particular manner with his work of salvation, to make it present and effective everywhere in the world. Saint Jean-Marie Vianney went so far as to say, 'Without the priest, the death and passion of our Lord would be of no use. It is the priest who continues the work of Redemption on earth.' It is this that we must put into effect: it is, accordingly, not our work, but the design of the Father and salvific work of the Son. The Holy Spirit makes use of our mind, of our mouth, of our hands. It is our especial task to proclaim the Word unceasingly, in order to spread the gospel, and to translate it in such a way that we touch people's hearts without altering it or diminishing it; and it is ours to perform once again the offering that Jesus made at the Last Supper and his acts of pardon for sinners…"[8]

At the Retreat given by Pope John Paul, there were Bishops and priests from over sixty countries. In what was once a small obscure village, the body of the canonised parish priest is venerated by pilgrims daily and visited by priests who seek to renew their own sense of vocation.

Pope Benedict XVI has spoken, like Pope John Paul II, of a "new springtime" in the Church and highlighted the role of the New Movements and communities, a sign of hope and new growth. In his letter about St John Vianney, he emphasised the role of a priest, quoting Vianney's own beautiful words on the subject. A priest is not there for himself – he is for others. He brings Christ to the people.

> "Dear brother priests, let us ask the Lord Jesus for the grace to learn for ourselves something of the pastoral plan of Saint John Mary Vianney! The first thing we need to learn is the complete identification of the man with his ministry. In Jesus, person and mission tend to coincide: all Christ's saving activity was, and is, an expression of his 'filial consciousness' which from all eternity stands before the Father in an attitude of loving submission to his will. In a humble yet genuine way, every priest must aim for a similar identification."[9]

St John Vianney has long been patron saint of parish priests, and as part of the Year for Priests, he will be announced as patron saints of all priests, working in every field – in hospitals, schools, prisons, religious communities, missions.

John Vianney himself taught and explained the role of saints – as models of holiness, as intercessors in Heaven, and he insisted that holiness was something for which everyone should strive. "We can, if we will, become a saint, for God will never refuse to help us to do so." He liked to give examples of courage, faith, and endurance from the lives of saints, to show them as older brothers and sisters from whom inspiration could be drawn. The most important thing to remember is that Heaven is our true destination, and he showed this in an imagined dialogue with God:

"O my God, why have you sent me into the world?" "To save your soul." "And why do you wish me to save my soul?" "Because I love you."[10]

NOTES

1. Pope John Paul II, in a retreat given to priests at Ars, October 1986.
2. *The Curé d'Ars Today*, George William Rutler, Ignatius Press 1988.
3. Letter quoted in *The Curé d'Ars, portrait of a parish priest*, Lancelot Sheppard, London, Burns and Oates, 1958.

4. *The Curé d'Ars, portrait of a parish priest*, Lancelot Sheppard, London, Burns and Oates 1958.
5. *Sacerdoti Nostri Primordia*, Pope John XXXIII, 1959.
6. Pope John Paul II, Holy Thursday letter to priests, 1986.
7. Ibid.
8. Pope John Paul II, Retreat at Ars, First Meditation, 6 October 1986.
9. Pope Benedict XVI, 2009, letter announcing a "Year for Priests".
10. *Thoughts of the Curé d'Ars*, TAN Books USA.

BIBLIOGRAPHY

John Vianney, The Life and Times of the Cure of Ars, J.B. Midgley, London, Catholic Truth Society, 2008.

The Curé of Ars Today, George William Rutler, Ignatius Press, San Francisco, 1988.

The Curé d'Ars, portrait of a parish priest, Lancelot C. Sheppard, London, Burns and Oates, 1958.

The Curé of Ars and his Cross, Jean de la Varende, 1958

The Secret of the Curé d'Ars, Henri Gheon. London, Sheed and Ward, 1946.

Thoughts of the Curé D'Ars, TAN Books USA, 1984.

Sermons of the Curé of Ars, tr. Una Morrissey, 1960, current edition TAN Books USA.